The Appointment

Intercessory Prayer

by Jackie Thomas

The Appointment: Intercessory Prayer

© 2021 by Jackie Thomas

ISBN: 978-1-63073-391-9

Cover illustrator: Stacy Thomas

Contact the author through her email account:
morningbird1@yahoo.com

Published by:
Faithful Life Publishers • North Fort Myers, FL 33903
888.720.0950 • info@FaithfulLifePublishers.com
www.FaithfulLifePublishers.com

Published in the United States of America
25 24 23 22 21   1 2 3 4 5

DEDICATION

To Stacy and Jenny Thomas...thank you for always being here for me, supporting me with encouragement and love...I respect you for not always agreeing with me, instead you tell me the truth, not what you think I want to hear. I thank God for blessing me with you both! I love you!

INTRODUCTION

This book is for anyone and everyone that prays. It is especially for those who are unsure if they are hearing the Holy Spirit calling out to them to become intercessors.

This isn't the *normal* book on intercession, but it is what I felt in my heart to write.

Before I knew I was an intercessor, I went through a lot of trial and error, much of which could have been avoided if I had known a few of the things I will tell you about on the pages of this book.

Some of you are called to be intercessors. Some are not.

All are told by Jesus to pray.

I am hoping this book will help you as you make your transition from WONDERING if you are called to be an Intercessor, to KNOWING you are a called Intercessor, and then DOING what you have been called to do!

I have tried to be obedient as I attempted to show that Intercessors are "real" people, not super spiritual Christians that do everything right or know all about praying!

I'm sure you will notice pretty quick that I am not super anything, unless it is super blessed!

We are human. We make mistakes. We fail!

But we also learn! And we grow…and we must never quit or give up!

Because eventually we realize it isn't *us*, that it is God's Spirit working through us!

God is looking for a willing and obedient heart, not a perfect vessel! Thank you, God, or I would have been on the 'cut' list!

It is my hope that by being as transparent as I possibly can in relating some of my experiences to you, that it will help you realize God will use anyone, in any circumstance, to pray for others. He not only can, but He will.

God does not call the qualified, but He qualifies those He calls!

I don't know as much as I would like to about intercession. I am still learning. My prayer is that by sharing what I DO know and have experienced, it will encourage others to accept the call.

I will be praying for you as you enter the realm of the Spirit, heart to heart, with the God of the Universe.

****

Clear your mind, ready your heart, bow quietly before God.

Think about WHO He is.

He is GOD

He is Jehovah-Rapha, the Lord that Heals, El-Elyon, the God Most High, Almighty, Omnipresent, Omnipotent, the God with Unlimited Power, the God that can do absolutely ANYTHING!

There is NOTHING impossible for God!

Let that sink into…not just your brain…but into your heart.

He created you, not from a mold, but you, individually—exactly how He wanted you to be.

Be Still.

He is drawing near to you.

Wait on Him.

Anticipate His Presence.

Enter into His Love, His Peace,
His Protection, His Provision.

The Name of the Lord is a Strong Tower,
the Righteous run to it and are safe.

Rest in Him.

Place your heart with all of its worry
and cares on the Mercy Seat.

Walk away.

Leave them there in His hands.

Don't look back.

It's done.

We can do nothing of ourselves.

Prayer with Faith works.

TABLE OF CONTENTS

CHAPTER 1

WHAT IF...

Talk about flakey! Yep, that should have been my middle name, or maybe even my first name!

Today I think I will finally begin writing the book I **know** I'm supposed to be writing. So I write...and delete...and write...and delete and... Ok, so maybe today *wasn't* the day I was supposed to start. Tomorrow I will for sure...

Do you feel that way about anything in your life? Please tell me I am not the only one that ever feels that way! But, just in case you do, would you like to sit here with me and talk awhile?

What if it isn't about writing a book?

What if it's about starting a project?

Or *what if* it's about getting out more to visit people that need you? And yes, there are people that need you!

Whatever the "what if" is, if you are like me, your best intentions don't always work out.

Here's something to consider.

What if your worry is that you will get started doing whatever it is, and then just let it go...again? There's a word for that, and no, it isn't lazy, but it might be lack of confidence or fear. Maybe even both.

Fear. Now that's a real one. Fear of being laughed at, Fear that it isn't really God that has put this on your heart, and yes, Fear of failing. Just so you know, there is NO failure in praying, ever!

Ok, *what if* it's just that you don't know how to get started, or what to do once you actually take that first step?

So, what about Intercession? That's kind of scary isn't it? There's a lot of commitment involved!

What if your knees aren't up to all that kneeling?

What if God won't listen to you?

And then there's all those people that need you to pray…*what if* you just fall asleep?

What if it's all in your mind?

What if it's only you that think you should be an intercessor?

WOW! That's a lot of *what ifs*!

Now, take a minute and think about these "what ifs".

What if you could *know* if you are called to be an intercessor?

What if it isn't all about kneeling or knowing "what to pray"?

What if Jesus did it all on the cross and you just have to remind God of what has already been done?

What if we read on and check out some of these *What ifs*.

CHAPTER 2

PRAYER AND GOD'S WORD

Prayer is talking *with* God, not just *to* Him. In prayer we seek His heart and open our own heart to Him.

There are many, many examples of prayer in the Bible. They are good guidelines on how we should pray but each one of us needs to pray the way the Holy Spirit leads us to.

When I am in my 'prayer place', it's only God and me. God knows me and I know Him. Well, He knows me better than I do Him, but I am working on knowing Him more!

I can't speak for you, but when I first got saved, I was really 'gung-ho' for God!

Yep, I wanted to do everything right! I would go into my 'prayer closet' and pray what I thought would please God. Not that pleasing God is a bad thing, but I would only show Him the face I wanted Him to see…the *good* side of me.

Really, I didn't even have a good side, just a side that wanted to please God, so I lied to Him by trying to deceive Him into thinking I was someone I was not! Lie to God?

Pretty obvious I didn't really know God or that He sees my heart! What was I thinking!!

I didn't really pray that much anyway but the occasional "Oh God, I need Your help" moment would come along, and I would fall on my knees and pour out my heart to Him! I need this…Help…I need that type of praying!

After one of those times of 'desperate' prayer, I finished by saying "I love you God." I always said that to God after praying. (you know, the good side of me showing through).

Only this time I heard a soft whisper speak very loudly to my heart…" Do you?" What? Why would I think a thought like that? Of course I love God…uh, of course I love You God!

Well you know how the Holy Spirit works. I would be going along with my "daily doings" and then this random thought would shatter my "happy go luckys" …" why would God ask me that?"

Then the thought "maybe it wasn't even God". Maybe it was Satan trying to make me think I don't love God! About three seconds after that thought popped into my mind, I laughed! I might have been born (again) yesterday but I know if it was Satan, he would be telling me God didn't love me, not that I didn't love God! Pretty sure he would have just let that one slide.

So what did I do? I got down on my knees and got honest with my Father. I explained that I wanted to love Him. That I did love what He had done for me, that He willingly died for me.

But that I wasn't really sure if thankful and grateful meant I actually loved Him? And that was hard to say to God!

I asked Him to help me…no bawling and squalling like my desperate prayers, just Him and I talking. I told Him I wanted a meaningful relationship with Him. That when I said 'I love you' to Him, I wanted it to come from my heart, not my head. Not just because I was thankful for my salvation, and especially not because that was what I thought I should say to my Creator!

I didn't want to hear Him say "Do you?" ever again!

I truly believe my Father smiled and said, Ok, *now* we can have that kind of relationship.

I began by asking Him to forgive me and thanked Him for showing me I was being deceptive. I wasn't purposely lying to Him. I believe at first, I loved the 'concept' of a loving God, but now I truly love Him! Next, I opened my Bible and began studying God's character and learning what pleases Him and what does not! What does all this have to do with intercession? How can we petition God, ask Him for anything, if we don't know Him? Or know His Word?

We need to spend time and effort for that relationship to become strong.

Take a walk with Him. Talk with Him about things you see as you are walking, tell Him about your ideas, dreams or just thank Him for who He is in your life. And listen, He will speak to your heart.

God says to us, come to Me and you will recover your life. I'll show you how to rest. Take a walk with Me, keep company with Me.

An important part of our effective prayer life is our "intimate" relationship with God, Jesus and the Holy Spirit.

They have three distinct personalities that join together and make One Godhead. They work independently in our lives, and at the same time work together as One.

As we study God's Word, we'll get to know all three of the Trinity. We will learn what God's Will is. And once we know Them, and God's Word is strong in us, He will hear, and answer our prayers.

Jesus said, *"If you abide in Me, and My Words abide in you, you will ask what you desire, and it shall be done for you."* **(John 15:7)**

I John 5:14-15 says it very clearly. *"Now, this is the confidence that we have in Him, that if we ask anything according to His Will, He hears us. And if we know that He hears us, whatever we ask, we know that we have the petitions that we have asked of Him."*

Once we know **what** God's Word says, we can then pray according to His Will and **know** that He has heard our prayer. It **shall** be done for us. Simple truth. He said it will!

In scripture, when we see the word "shall", it is an absolute. *Not* maybe, or it might happen, but absolutely! It will begin to be, to come into existence, it shall happen!

So as we study and learn His Word and His character, our life should become ***His Word put into practice.*** It should be our way of life in any situation.

When we speak it should be His Word that comes out of our heart and mouth. "*A good man out of the good treasure of his heart brings forth good; and an evil man out of the evil treasure of his heart brings forth evil; for out of the abundance of the heart his mouth speaks.*" **Luke 6:45**

Whatever we do or say should be a reflection of Him and His love.

His Word alive in us, His Word working through us!

Any darkness in our soul needs to be filled with the Light of God's Word and the Holy Spirit.

To Abide in Him, we **R**ead His Word, **O**bey His Word, **L**earn His Word, and **L**ive His Word! So...Let's ROLL! I'm having a T-Shirt made with that on it! Want one?

CHAPTER 3

… AND I PRAY

"Search me, O God, and know my heart, try me and know my thoughts; and see if there be any wicked way in me, and lead me in the way everlasting. **Psalm 139:23-24** KJV **We** have to be real with God. He knows our hearts and personality.

Prayer doesn't have to be *long* for God to hear it.

Or loud…

Or elegant…

It just needs to be from *your heart*!

Learn scripture so you can pray God's Will in any situation. Learn it and fill your heart with it, and when it is needed, it will be there!

Ask the Holy Spirit to bring it to your remembrance, to remind you of what His Word says. His Word confirms that He will do just that!

John 14:26 KJV says this – *"But the comforter, which is the Holy Ghost, whom the Father will send in my name, He shall teach you all things, and bring all things to your remembrance whatsoever I have said unto you."*

When we know God's Word and speak it into a situation, we are speaking His Will into it.

"And this is the confidence that we have in Him, that if we ask any thing according to His Will, He hears us, and if we know that He hears us, whatever we ask, we know that we have the petitions we have asked of Him." That's **I John 5:14-15**

Not our opinion. Not our concerns. Not even our interpretation of it!

Just speak God's Word!

"So is my Word that goes out from my mouth: It will not return to Me empty, but will accomplish what I desire and achieve the purpose for which I sent it". **Isaiah 55:11** NIV

"For the Word of God is living and powerful, and sharper than any two-edged sword, piercing even to the division of soul and spirit, and of joints and marrow, and is a discerner of the thoughts and intents of the heart." **Hebrews 4:12**

His Word judges the ***attitude*** of our hearts!

Even the 'driest' prayer, when you are speaking the Word of God, will break down strongholds and bring victory! Why? Because it is the <u>*Word of God*</u> and the <u>*Spirit of God*</u> that brings it into reality!

Isaiah 40:8 KJV *"The grass withereth,, the flower fadeth but the Word of our God shall stand forever."* Notice the word *shall*!

We need to know who we are in Christ and that we can *"come boldly to the throne of grace, (with our petitions) that we may obtain mercy and find grace in our time of need."* That's found in **Hebrews 4:16.**

Remember as intercessors, we are 'standing in place of' those who need His help in their time of need.

God's Will is revealed in His Word so we don't need to pray "If it is Your Will". When we know His Word, we can pray BECAUSE it is Your Will!

And then expect the answer! Not with haughtiness or demanding, but with the humble assurance that comes from *knowing* our Father *has* heard and *will* give whatever we have asked!

When we speak God's Word into any situation, there is no failure. It is the Word of God and the Spirit of God that brings it into reality. So, once again, we need to know His Word!

Praying in the Holy Ghost is essential and powerful! I know some may not like that statement, but really, if you have a problem with it, you will have to take that up with God…He's the one that said it!

Romans 8:26-27 *"Likewise the Spirit also helps in our weaknesses. For we do not know what we should pray for as we ought, but the Spirit Himself makes intercession for us with groanings which cannot be uttered. Now He who searches the hearts knows what the mind of the Spirit is, because He makes intercession for the saints according to the Will of God."*

Jesus Himself told the disciples, *"But you shall receive power when the Holy Spirit has come upon you.*" **Acts 1:8** It goes on to say in **Acts 2:4** KJV *"And they were all filled with the Holy Ghost and began to speak with other tongues as the Spirit gave them utterance."* They began declaring the wonders of God!

There is power when you pray in the Holy Ghost!

We can pray in our own understanding and in our own language. We also can pray in the Spirit, pray in tongues, or an unknown language to us.

Here is what the Word says about it. *"What is the conclusion then? I will pray with the Spirit and I will also pray with the understanding. I will sing with the Spirit, and I will also sing with understanding.*" **I Corinthians 14:15**

Sometimes you will find you begin praying in your known language only to flow into speaking an unknown one. Let me say this, it is unknown to us, but very known to God!

Please, if you have doubts, study His Word and ask God to open your mind to the truth in the scriptures.

"Then opened He their understanding, that they could understand the scriptures." **Luke 24:45** KJV

Jesus said.... *"If ye continue in My Word, then ye are My disciples indeed; and you shall know the truth, and the truth shall make you free."* **John 8: 31-32** KJV

CHAPTER 4

WHAT *IS* THIS THING CALLED INTERCESSION

First, let me say, *EVERYONE* is supposed to pray.

The Word says this…" *Therefore I exhort first of all those supplications, prayers, intercessions, and giving of thanks be made for all men, for Kings and all who are in authority, that we may lead a quiet and peaceable life in all godliness and reverence."* **I Timothy 2:1-2**

Jesus said in **Luke 18:1** *"Then He spoke a parable to them that men always ought to pray and not lose heart"*

I Thessalonians 5:16-18 says, *"Rejoice always, pray without ceasing, in everything give thanks; for this is the will of God in Christ Jesus for you."*

God wants everyone to be saved and come to the saving knowledge of Jesus.

But not *EVERYONE* is called to be an Intercessor.

"For I wish that all men were even as I myself. But each one has his own gift from God, one in this manner and another in that." **I Corinthians 7:7**

The scripture goes on to say in **I Corinthians 12: 4-6**, *"There are different kinds of gifts but the same Spirit. There are differences of ministries but the same Lord. And there are differsities of activities, but it is the same God who works all in all."*

I Corinthians 12:18 says, *"But now God has set the members, each one of them, in the body, just as He pleased."*

Every gift and calling is important to the body of Christ and the unsaved world. God has placed every one of us exactly where He wants us to be. Albeit some of us put up a lot of resistance but God knows where He wants us to be, and where we will best serve Him and the body of Christ.

Intercessors are not important people in themselves, BUT they are people with an important job to do! That's worth saying twice don't you think?

Webster's dictionary defines an Intercessor as "a person that goes before God in prayer on behalf of another person, situation or circumstance."

An intercessor knows that nothing that they do can change anything.

In John 5:30, Jesus says, *"I can of myself do nothing, as I hear, I judge, and my judgment is righteous."*

We seek to know God's heart. We pray, *"thy* will be done, not *my* will be done."

Jesus continued in **John 5:30** saying, *"because I do not seek My own Will, but the Will of My Father who sent Me."*

We understand the power in prayer comes totally through Jesus. We know it is the *completed* work of Jesus on the cross and the power of His Blood and His Name!

Jesus sits at the right hand of God, ever making intercession for us! *"Who is he who condemns? It is Christ who died, and furthermore is also risen, who is even at the right hand of God, who also makes intercession for us."* **Romans 8:34**

"Therefore He is also able to save to the uttermost those who come to God through Him, since He always lives to make intercession for them." **Hebrews 7:25**

Intercessors *are not* attention seekers. That is not to say that there will never be a time when you will boldly do battle, out loud, in the

Spirit, with demonic forces! If you are not alone that will tend to draw attention, but it should not be the pray-er seeking attention. God does not cause confusion, but He has been known to be pretty 'showy' at times! Always be led by His Holy Spirit.

Ephesians 6:12 KJV *"For we wrestle not against flesh and blood, but against principalities, against powers, against the rulers of the darkness of this world, against spiritual wickedness in high places."*

As intercessors, we are constantly battling the dark side of the spirit world. When we see a fellow intercessor gripped in battle with dark forces, we need to surround them in prayer, and intercede for them. Not interrupt or interfere, just cover them in prayer. We can, and need to bind and cast away any oppressive spirits and petition God to send His angels to surround and protect the one praying and the one being prayed for.

"For He shall give His angels charge over you, to keep you in all your ways." **Psalm 91:11**

All intercessors need someone to pray for them on a consistent, daily basis. We need the prayer covering protection of another Pray-er. If you don't have someone that will be *committed* to pray for you daily, ask God to send you someone.

CHAPTER 5

BURDEN BEARER

We have all more than likely heard someone say they felt "burdened" to pray for someone or to pray for a certain situation. Or maybe you haven't. So what is a Burden?

A Burden is something you feel intense responsibility to pray for. It may be a person, a situation, or an event. Anything God wants you to pray for.

When God has placed a Burden on you to pray, you will feel the intensity of the need until you are 'released'. Sometimes you will feel a temporary 'lifting' of the need to pray, only to have it return later on. I have no idea why; I just know that it certainly does. More important though is just to continue praying until the burden finally lifts for good. You will know. There is no time limit to pray. The Holy Spirit will guide you. Some burdens last a long time while others are short.

Unfortunately a burden doesn't usually come at a *convenient* time to pray. Life and death are not convenient!

But I *have* learned over time that I *can* pray anywhere, anytime.

Picture this… a beautiful new powdery snow had fallen this particular morning. So, of course, EVERYONE that could possibly get to the slopes, had made their way to the little mountain town in Colorado. And, at least, ALL of them, had stopped at the fast-food place where I worked as a cashier, so they could have a good breakfast before the fun began. Smiling, ringing up the order, here's your change, have a great day, repeat…my morning seemed to be going smoothly and all was well in my world. Remember the very soft voice that I heard so loudly before? I heard the voice of the Holy Spirit say to pray for the young man with the motorcycle helmet in his hand. Yep, the young man that had just stepped up to my register.

Now Lord? With at least half of the town in line behind him? And, really, he looks pretty healthy and happy to me God!

Nope, I didn't say any of that but when I handed the young man his receipt, I silently asked God for His protection and wisdom in this young man's life. That His perfect Will would come to pass. I didn't need to 'lay hands' on him or make a big deal out of it, just pray silently in my mind.

Did I ever see the result to that prayer? Did I know what I needed to pray?

No, to both questions. But I knew beyond a shadow of a doubt that the prayer I prayed made a difference!

God doesn't waste anyone's time.

A good perspective on this is, if you were the one with the need, wouldn't you want an intercessor to begin praying as soon as they received the call from God?

Many more people came to my register that day, but the Lord didn't put anyone else on my heart to pray for.

God will always open the door for you to pray. Always expect an opening. He asked you to pray, He will make a way

CHAPTER 6

TALE-BEARER and GOSSIP

Psalm 141: 3 – *"Set a guard, O LORD, over my mouth; Keep watch over the door of my lips."*

Let's talk a little about Tale Bearer's, or as we commonly know them to be called – Gossips!

This subject cannot be stressed enough!

Most of us have been on the hurting end of gossip at least one time in our lives. Unfortunately, most of us have been on the other end of that nasty little road a time or two as well.

The Holy Spirit dealt mightily with me on gossip. It seems He and I had a whole different concept of what was gossip and what was a prayer request.

I always started off with good intentions, I really did, but would find myself sliding into a gray area, and we all know there are no gray areas with God.

For some reason just saying "I don't gossip" doesn't stop most people from trying to share their news with you anyway.

One way to stop people from trying to gossip with you goes something like this.

The names have been changed to protect the guilty…Suppose Nitpicky Nelda says, "Oh, there's Sally Sunshine. I'm so upset with her!

All she ever does is Smile!... Smile, Smile, Smile!! Doesn't she realize people can only stand a certain amount of smiling?"

Now, this gives me the opportunity to agree with Nitpicky and even add my own thoughts on the matter. "I know, right! You think she would know that smiling just leads to laughter and who knows from there!"

Or I could take Nitpicky by the arm saying, "I think we need to just go over there to Sally Sunshine so you can tell her those pearly whites of hers are beginning to blind you!" "Certainly once she understands how you are being offended, she will work with you to find a solution that will have you both smiling in no time!" About that time the problem will seem a lot less significant to Nitpicky and she will decline. Most often people would rather complain, and gossip than actually have the problem fixed.

The best answer I have found when I am offered the opportunity to gossip is just to say, "Let's pray and ask God for His Wisdom and perfect Will in this situation." And then do it!

And continue praying for the person or situation every day until you have the answer or the unction to stop.

What Satan intended for harm through tale bearing and gossip, has now been taken to God in prayer! What our enemy had intended for harm God will now turn to good!

God may tell you that Ms. Snooty Tooty is battling with pride and haughtiness but that does NOT mean He wants you to hop right in there and tell her what He said or how she can fix her problem!

Be careful to understand this.

The only reason He will ever show you anything is for that persons good. He doesn't want you to confront the person or 'fix' their problem.

That is not *your* job!

God DOES want you to pray for her, to stand in her place so He can minister His love to her.

God DOES want you to STAND between her and demonic forces, that are interfering with His plan for her life!

There is a fine line between gossip and prayer requests, so always be led by the Holy Spirit.

Anything an intercessor prays about is between God and that intercessor and NO ONE else!

Proverbs 11:13 *"A talebearer reveals secrets, but he who is of a faithful spirit conceals a matter."*

Leviticus 19:16 says, *"You shall not go about as a tale bearer among your people, nor shall you take a stand against the life of your neighbor; I am the LORD."*

I Timothy 5:13 – *"And besides they learn to be idle, wandering about from house to house, and not only idle but also gossips and busy bodies, saying things which they ought not."*

God is speaking of our *personal conduct.*

If you want to be an intercessor, then you cannot be a gossip or a tale bearer.

God needs to be able to trust you!

CHAPTER 7

DO YOUR BEST—
LEAVE THE REST TO GOD

As Pray-ers, we seek God and petition Him for answers to so many things! Sometimes it doesn't seem like He hears us. We need to remember that we can't 'make' things happen just because we believed they would or because God hears us.

People still have free will and still can choose their own destiny.

That is what is so awesome about our God! He loves us and He wants us to freely love Him back. Not to *have* to love Him back.

Although it breaks His heart when we chose the wrong path, He will not *make* us do anything!

I am going to compare your 'job' as an intercessor to working in a factory that assembles cars.

Part of that process is the seat belt. You get up every day and go to work. You have a job to do. And you love your job. You install seat belts into every vehicle that passes through your assembly line. You don't install seat belts in "every" vehicle in the world, just those that pass in front of you on your conveyer belt.

Day after day, week after week, month after month, year after year, you faithfully do your part to ensure every vehicle has a safety feature called the seatbelt.

Once you've completed your part of the process, the vehicle moves on to the next person, who then does their job.

Even though you've installed in-numerable seatbelts in vehicles over the years, you probably will never see *even* one of them put into use.

You won't see the parent when they buckle their child securely with the seat belt you installed. And you won't see people as they go about their daily lives, buckling up for safety...not to mention "Click it or Ticket."

But that doesn't mean they don't do it or it hasn't protected them or their loved ones. It doesn't mean you didn't install it properly.

You also won't see the people that were involved in wrecks, some minor, some horrific, and yet they were unharmed! They were protected from injury or even death because they fastened the seat belt you installed in their vehicle.

Then there are those that were injured and even killed because they chose not to fasten the seat belt, the very one you installed for their safety!

It was their choice!

No you won't see them either. That's not part of your job.

You installed the seat belt properly, and you believed it would do what it was designed to do. You don't wake up in the middle of the night worried that maybe the seat belt won't work properly...you trust that it will. You have done your job.

That's how intercessory prayer works. We don't quit praying if it doesn't seem like our prayers worked. We don't have to see the results of our prayers.

We trust God! Trust that He has heard and answered our prayers. Trust Him and His Holy Spirit to use our prayers to accomplish His Will in this earth.

We *know* the *"effectual fervent prayer of a righteous man avails much."* (**James 5:16**) And we *know "His Word will accomplish what He has sent it to do."*

God has given mankind free will. There are people who refuse the provision God has made for them. He does all that can be done, but in the end, it is still us that make the final decision.

Like the people that didn't use their seat belt, even though ALL they had to do was reach down and fasten it, they chose not to.

We chose either to listen to God, or turn away.

CHAPTER 8

THE ASSIGNMENT

As you grow in your responsibilities as an intercessor, you may be given an assignment. An assignment being someone or some situation God wants you to specifically intercede for.

There are various ways to receive your assignment.

There is no set way. I have named a few but always remember God will do it however it pleases Him and the way He chooses will probably not even be on this list. His ways are not our ways. **Isaiah 55:8** *"For My thoughts are not your thoughts nor are your ways My ways," says the Lord.*

One way you might receive an assignment is through prayer. Another is receiving a word through one of God's prophets.

Still another and I know this has happened to most of us at some time or another, is someone's name or face keeps popping into our mind.

Sometimes it's just a random thought brought on by some jogged memory. But oftentimes it's the Holy Spirit bringing you an assignment.

Always pray and find out.

Have you ever been watching the news and knew you needed to pray for someone you saw on there?

 Maybe it's a person in a television commercial and you prayed for them for months after?

Here's one you'll love…how about that jerk that cuts *you* off while you're driving and then honks, giving *you* the famous salute?

Praying for him might have stopped road rage on down the road!

Did you ever stop to consider that you might be the only person that's praying for some of these people?

Receiving a prayer assignment is sort of like…Ding! you've got mail…from God!

Quite a few years back, my husband and I were attending a Bible Study at our church. Our son, John had recently started going also so we would just swing by his house on our way, and we would all ride together. Same plan this night, except he wasn't waiting at the end of the drive when we stopped by to pick him up. No big deal.

We continued on to the study. This is pretty boring so far, right?

But this story actually starts earlier in the day when I was cleaning, (still boring) and the Holy Spirit spoke to my heart, saying, "Pray the 91st Psalm over John."

I knew that meant I needed to pray.

I did kind of mention to God that I had just seen John and he looked ok to me. But nonetheless, I began praying the 91st Psalm over every part of John's life.

As the day progressed, I felt impressed several more times to pray the 91st Psalm for John but especially verses 14 and 15.

By the time our Bible Study was coming to a close, my assignment was fast becoming a burden! I explained to the members how I had been prompted by the Spirit to pray for John and we joined together once again to pray for him.

Ok, now back a few hours earlier. A couple of John's friends had stopped by his house in the friends new Jeep. They asked him to go for a ride to check it out, with promises of being back in time for the Bible Study. Being April in the mountains, there was still snow on the ground, but the roads were clear and in good condition. There was a lake a few miles out of town so off they went on their adventure.

The adventure soon went south becoming an accident instead!

Failure to negotiate a sharp curve plus striking a mile marker pole, the Jeep flipped, landing about 10 feet down in the icy water of the river, upside down!

The driver and his girlfriend were unhurt and managed to make it safely out and onto the snowy bank. When the Jeep overturned, John had been thrown out the side window and into the water.

The water was only a few feet deep, but the Jeep landed on John's back, pinning him face down under the water!

Unable to get the Jeep off of him, and in pretty much of a panic, John's friends left him there to try and get help.

They later estimated it took about 45 minutes to find anyone since houses were few and far between in the country. When they returned with help, there on the bank... soaked, muddy and cold sat John!

He didn't have a clue how he had gotten out from under the Jeep and onto the shore.

The last thing he remembered was struggling to get free and thinking, "I should have gone to the Bible Study...God I don't want to die like this, help me please!"

Back in those days we didn't have cell phones, so we used 'land lines' and pay phones. Surely some of you remember pay phones?

Anyway back then a payphone booth was pretty easy to find, and I still had un-easiness about my son so we found a booth so I could call our pastor.

We had barely said hello when the operator interrupted the call, explaining to pastor that his number had been listed as a number to call in case of emergency.

She went on to say John had been in an accident and the hospital was trying to reach my husband and I.

I do not believe in coincidence! God had timed it by the Holy Spirit prompting me to call pastor exactly at the time the operator would be trying to reach him.

We lived about 15 miles from the pastor, and we did not have a phone. If the operator had contacted him when we were not on the phone, he would have had to get out of bed, dress and drive to our house to let us know!

God is awesome!!

By the time the ambulance arrived to transport John to the hospital it had been well over 5 hours since the accident. Yet he did not have hypothermia as you would expect.

He was admitted to the hospital and released a few days later.

At first we were told he had damage to his kidney where the roll bar from the Jeep had landed on him. And they were watching to be sure he didn't get pneumonia from the water and mud being in his lungs.

Despite all the tests and initial diagnosis, the Dr. said they could find no injuries, even his lungs were clear!

Oh, he did have one minor injury, a bruise where the roll bar of the Jeep had pinned him under the icy cold water!

That is an example of an assignment.

Thinking back I remembered **Psalm 91 verse 14 – 15** says, *"Because he has set his love upon Me, therefore I will deliver him." "He shall call upon Me and I will answer him. I will be with him in trouble; I will deliver him and honor him."*

What if I hadn't listened to the Holy Spirit when he prompted me to pray? After all, I knew he was ok and I was busy with my 'boring' day. I could have easily said, "It's probably not God…probably just me.

Maybe God would have given, or maybe had already given the assignment to others as well. And what if they had also said …It's probably just me or been too busy? I don't know.

Ezekiel 22:30 KJV – *And I sought for a man among them that should make up the hedge, and stand in the gap before me for the land, that I should not destroy it, but I found none.* God was looking for someone to take His assignment.

Always Pray!!

CHAPTER 9

PRAISE OR WARRIOR INTERCESSOR

A Praise Intercessor enters into spiritual battle with the Word of God coming forth from their mouth in Praise!

I've had many Praise intercessors say they feel like other types of intercession are more important than theirs! I wonder if that's because they enjoy their calling so much, they just can't believe it is so important!

It's my personal belief the Praise Intercessors are the first line of defense in great spiritual battles!

Remember, God inhabits and/or dwells in Praise! So when the Prais-er is Praising that's when the Creator of ALL things, the ONE TRUE GOD, the King of all Kings, is right there among them!

Walls are broken down; barriers are destroyed, and demons flee from the Presence of Almighty God!

II Chronicles 20:14-22 -NIV "The spirit of the Lord spoke to the people through Jahaziel. He said, *"Listen King Jehoshaphat and all who live in Judah and Jerusalem. "this is what the Lord says to you. Do not be afraid or discouraged because of this vast army. For the battle is not yours but God's."* **Verse 17** says, *"You will not have to fight this battle. Take up your positions; stand firm and see the deliverance the Lord will give you, O Judah and Jerusalem. Do not be afraid; Do not be discouraged. Go out to face them tomorrow, and the Lord will be with you."*

God is saying to us as well…Do not be afraid or discouraged because of this trial, sickness, disease or whatever has come against you. For the battle is not ours but God's!

God is saying to the Praise Intercessor… Stand firmly in your position and let your Praise be heard!

Verse 18 and 19 show that all the people fell down and worshipped before the Lord…and *they Praised the Lord with a very loud voice*!

Now look at verse 21. *"After consulting the people, Jehoshaphat appointed men to **sing** to the Lord and to **Praise** Him for the splendor of His Holiness, as they **went out at the head of the army**!*

The Praise-ers were saying, Give thanks to the Lord, (Praise Him) for His Mercy (Love) endures forever!

Did you notice the Praise-ers were the first in the line, at the head of the army? They were in front of everyone!

The soldiers (Warrior Intercessors) were next.

When you read the rest of the story you will see the enemy was completely destroyed!

But it was a *joint effort* by all! Praise intercessors enter into the realm of the Spirit in many different ways. They come into the battle with boldness, with gentleness, and with perseverance, just naming a few. Walls of protection are established! God enters their Praise and the enemy cannot stand!

I have yet to meet a Praise intercessor that doesn't wake up with a song in their mind, and more often than not, with a song on their lips…out loud!

Often times, my friend, who is a Praise Intercessor, will wake up from a sound sleep to the sound of her voice singing Praise to God. Her spirit was Praising God while she still slept!

"Let the saints be joyful in glory: let them sing aloud upon their beds." **Psalm 149:5** KJV

The following are just a few of the scriptures that describe Praise intercession.

"Let the high Praises of God be in their mouth and a two edged sword in their hands." **Psalm 149:6** KJV

"But thou art Holy, O thou that inhabits the Praises of Israel." **Psalm 22:3** KJV

"Praise ye the LORD. Praise the LORD O my soul. While I live will I Praise the LORD; I will sing Praises unto my God, while I have any being." **Psalm 146:1-2** KJV

A Warrior intercessor fights the same battle only in a different way. They are just the opposite of the Prais-er, who is Joyful, full of Worship and Praise.

Warriors travail in their spirit, sometimes loudly, sometimes with bold authority, other times quietly, even weeping. The Spirit will pray with groanings which cannot be uttered.

Romans 8:26 – *"Likewise the Spirit also helps in our weaknesses. For we do not know what we should pray for as we ought, but the Spirit Himself makes intercession for us with groanings which cannot be uttered."*

The Warrior enters the dark realm with the same Sword of the Spirit as the Praise intercessor, with the same Armor of God.

Both come in the Power of the Holy Spirit and the Word of God.

Both enter with Faith as their Shield. *"Finally, my brethren, be Strong in the Lord and in the Power of His Might."*

It is in Him that we find our strength and from His might that we receive power.

"Put on the whole armor of God that you may be able to stand against the wiles of the devil. For we wrestle not against flesh and blood, but against principalities, against powers, against the rulers of the darkness of this world, against spiritual wickedness in high places."

"Wherefore take unto you the whole armor of God that you will be able to withstand in the evil day, and having done all, to stand."

"Stand, therefore, having your loins girt about with the truth and having on the breastplate of righteousness. And your feet shod with the preparation of the gospel of peace."

"Above all, taking the Shield of Faith, wherewith you shall be able to quench all the fiery darts of the wicked."

"And take the Helmet of Salvation, and the Sword of the Spirit, which is the Word of God. "

"Praying always, with all prayer and supplication in the Spirit, and watching thereunto with all perseverance and supplication for all saints." **Ephesians 6:10-18** KJV

With this in mind, be alert and always keep on praying! Once again, praying in the Holy Spirit is essential and powerful!

CHAPTER 10

HABAKKUK

Habakkuk 2:1 *"I will stand my watch and set myself on the rampart, and watch to see what He will say to me, and what I will answer when I am corrected.* (note: a rampart is a defensive wall).

Near the end of the Old Testament, with only 3 chapters, is the Book of Habakkuk, the Prophet.

Habakkuk, unlike other prophets, didn't speak to the people about God, he spoke to God about the people.

He had questioned what God was doing and was waiting for God's answer. We won't always see the answer, but there is ALWAYS an answer. Habakkuk was expecting an answer.

I believe there is a little bit of Habakkuk's attitude in all of us, don't you? I know I have questioned God and wondered why the answer was taking so long!

God's answer to Habakkuk was 'wait'! If your answer seems slow in coming – wait – it's on the way.

And as always with God, the answer won't be too soon, and it won't be too late, it will be right on time! His time! Habakkuk had a relationship with God. He knew God's personality and he knew God's heart. He wasn't questioning the *correctness* of what God was doing. He was saying, God I don't understand this – this doesn't seem like the God I know…and God explained it to him.

Habakkuk realized that God *must* bring the judgment!

And then while on his knees, Habakkuk asked of God *"in wrath to remember mercy!"* **Habakkuk 3:2** (KJV)

As I said, he had a real relationship with God and knew God's personality.

God desires mercy, even in times of judgment.

So, even in the midst of all the suffering and famine, for there was no blessing on the land or the people, what did Habakkuk do?

He sang Praise to God and put his trust in God! Why? Because he knew God's heart, he had talked to Him about it, he had waited for his answer, and *regardless* of situations or circumstances, he KNEW God had heard his prayers and would DO WHAT HE SAID HE WOULD DO!!

Habakkuk was not only God's prophet, but he was also an Intercessor!

Habakkuk praised, trusted, prayed, sought God's heart, petitioned God's mercy, waited and believed!!

CHAPTER 11

AND THEN THERE IS THIS...

Sometimes when we pray, we know exactly what we are praying about, more often than not, we won't. Actually our spirit man does know since we are praying God's heart, but our carnal man does not.

The day I received this particular burden I had been praying corporately with my fellow intercessors and our pastor, Derek Heldreth, pastor of Christian Center Church in Norman Oklahoma. Corporate prayer is where a group of pray-ers join together in one mind and voice. We met as a group once a week but not to pray for personal needs. The time was set aside specifically to hear from God and then to pray His heart.

We would usually begin by praying for those in authority over us, leaders in government, first responders, teachers and many, many others.

I Timothy 2:1-4 *"Therefore I exhort first of all that supplications, prayers, intercessions, and giving of thanks be made for all men, for Kings and all who are in authority, that we may lead a quiet and peaceable life in all godliness and reverence. For this is good and acceptable in the sight of God our Savior, who desires all men to be saved and to come to the knowledge of truth."*

We were nearing the end of our prayer time, when I became overwhelmed with a heaviness in my spirit, more than I could withstand on my own. Falling in a crumpled heap on the carpet, I became engulfed in deep travail, speaking out loud divine intervention and protection, although I had no idea for whom or what the circumstance might be.

The other intercessors gathered around, covering and surrounding me with prayer, sensing the foreboding and darkness that I was battling.

After much warfare in the spirit realm by all of us, the burden began to lessen and finally lifted. After the others had gone, I asked Pastor Derek about what I had 'seen in the spirit', but he didn't know what it meant either. He suggested I continue to pray about it, which I did.

For several weeks I would enter the same dark realm in intercession in which I 'felt' an overwhelming intensity of fear and terror. I still had no idea what I prayed about.

This is what I saw…There were 2 airplanes flying near and towards very tall buildings, one ahead of the other. I saw another plane, but it was in open space.

That was all there was and yet what I 'saw' terrified me! The fear and despair I felt are not something I can easily describe in words!

An intercessor stands in the place for another, so quite often you will 'feel' the emotions connected with the person. Sometimes you will even feel the pain another is experiencing.

It is always a good idea to ask Holy Spirit about a sudden change in your feelings or comfort. As you grow as an intercessor you will be able to discern if what you are feeling is "yours" or if you need to intercede.

A few months passed and I was no longer praying about the airplanes or what I had felt. I didn't feel the urging by the Spirit to do so.

Then on September 11, 2001, the Twin Towers in New York City, were attacked by terrorists…in airplanes! I knew immediately in my spirit that I had been praying about that attack!

So many, many times in the days following the attack, I wept before God, broken hearted, my thoughts being that maybe I could have prayed more!

It was a horrible time, spiritually devastating!

I searched my heart…Had I missed God? What had I not done?

My job was to pray…my life was to pray…to stand in the gap, to take the place of others…and look how many had died!

We learn, or at least we have the opportunity to learn, from every experience we have, whether it be good or bad. I learned a great lesson from this one!

When you are an intercessor, the enemy will try to destroy you through "his" thoughts, which he will happily place in your mind if he finds an opening.

It is my belief that Intercessors rank way up there on Satan's 'hit' list!

After much soul searching, I was finally quiet, just listening for the voice of my Father. That is when I heard Holy Spirit speak to my heart.

This is what He said, "Father God did not give you the "Twin Towers" as your assignment. He gave you "someone" as your assignment!"

A multitude of intercessors had received the call from the Holy Spirit to pray, not just me. That was pretty humbling. And it also brought me great peace.

Many, many people were supernaturally snatched from the hand of death that day! *Intercessors* had answered the call to pray, travailing, seeking God's protection and divine intervention.

Intercessors had answered the call to Praise, thanking and worshipping God, breaking the walls so the battle could begin!

All of them bringing about God's perfect Will in the lives of people and in the situation that day.

Souls received salvation as well.

We've heard stories about people that overslept that morning, or their car wouldn't start. Or the one that thought, hey, I should bring donuts to my friends today, and stopped to pick them up, thus causing them to be a few minutes late, thus they were not in the building when it was hit by the plane.

Report after report about people that miraculously were able to escape the building! And the emergency responders with amazing accounts of what they said could only have been divine intervention. God knew who would be there and who He didn't want there. He also knew that human beings have a free will, and if they didn't heed the urging of His Holy Spirit, it would be their choice. I do know this. He is God…and our good is always first on His mind. One more thought…how many were divinely placed there that day because their whole life had been leading to that very moment? That moment when they would lead another to Salvation! Just moments before they both stepped into eternity!

Isn't our ultimate destination Heaven with our Lord?

What a glorious way to enter into our Lord's presence, by bringing the person with you that just received eternal life, because you told them about Jesus!

We must always be obedient to God, no matter the situation.

CHAPTER 12

AM I CALLED TO BE
AN INTERCESSOR

Now for the question we all ask ourselves at least once. Am I called to be an intercessor? First, ask God. He knows the answer and wants you to know as well! No one but the Holy Spirit can really tell you.

There are some things common to the calling of Intercessor. You may have heard the joke, "You might be a Red Neck if" and then it goes on to say some pretty funny reasons why you might.

Well, you might be an Intercessor if...

You love to pray. That seems kind of like...Well, thank you Captain Obvious. But it really isn't.

It's hard to believe, at least to an Intercessor, but there are actually people that don't feel comfortable praying or even really like to pray.

I know a lot of people that have a hard time saying a prayer of thanks to God for their food at mealtime. The other side to that is the person that prays two days-worth of prayer at mealtime because it's the *only* time they pray.

You might be an Intercessor if...

You find yourself praying a LOT. Not necessarily on your knees, crying out to God type of prayers. (although, those would be a pretty sure sign)

But when you hear a siren, do you say that silent prayer for whoever is involved?

A lot of us do that, but you take it a little farther, and pray for the emergency personnel, the driver of the emergency vehicle to be protected and not be involved in an accident, for people to pull over and yield to the emergency vehicles, fire truck, ambulance, police cars, tow trucks…and the families of those injured, for peace of mind and, and, and…pretty soon you have prayed for everyone's family and possibly generations to come.

You might be an Intercessor if…

You pass a teenager in the store or on the street, and read the look of anger, confusion, hurt, fear…any number of emotions on their face. Or you see nothing, you just feel compassion for our youth that have so much going on nowadays. You pray against the struggles they will face and speak protection while they are in school, and help for them to stand strong against the many temptations they face daily.

You might be an Intercessor if…

You are sitting on your sofa and your heart cries out, "Oh God, protect Jenny, she's so lost and making such bad decisions in her life! She needs You Lord! Send people across her path to help her see You and Your son Jesus and how much You love her… Oops! I remember I'm watching Forest Gump and Jenny is just a character…everyone does that, right? So I began to pray for the *real* people in the movie…You might be an Intercessor if…

How many times has an old friend or someone you don't even know that well, popped into your mind? Or just a name or a city or a country…here we go with the 'ors' again!

Pray for them!

Even if you are not an Intercessor, prayer won't hurt anyone!

Especially if it is someone you *don't like* or EVER *want* them popping into your mind.

Pray for them! God may be giving you the opportunity to forgive someone that you haven't forgiven!

I guarantee if it is Satan messing with you about someone that has caused you pain, if you pray for that person every time their name 'pops' into your 'head shed', it won't happen often!

Satan most definitely doesn't want you "praying" for your enemy!

God says to pray for our enemies and those who mistreat us. **Matthew 5:44** says this, "*But I say to you, love your enemies, bless those who hate you, and **pray** for those who spitefully use you and persecute you.*"

Those are just a few of the things that might lead you to believe you might be an Intercessor. As I said in the beginning, ask the Holy Spirit for guidance. And expect Him to give it.

And, since we are on the subject of forgiveness… Well, maybe we weren't exactly on that subject, but we are headed there now!

CHAPTER 13

FORGIVENESS IS NOT AN OPTION

If we expect God to hear our prayers, we have to forgive.

Forgiveness is not an option; it is a must!

It might help to remember that when we give forgiveness, it is really for our own sake, no one else's. It is a "God can't forgive me until I forgive you" sort of thing.

Here is the awesomeness of forgiveness! It doesn't mean they were 'right' doing whatever it was. It means that you love God enough to be obedient to His Word!

It means that you trust Him to bless you and forgive you.

Once again, you have an open door to enter into your Father's presence and see His prayer heart!

I have never, ever, hated anyone enough that they were worth giving up God or heaven for! No ONE!

And believe me, just as I am sure you have as well, I have *had* the opportunity!

Have you ever wondered why God says to pray for our enemies? I have...and I believe the reason is because He loves them, and because He loves us!

When we pray for anyone that has hurt us, lied to us, cheated us, or caused harm in any way, it will change things. Why?

First – prayer works! The person will begin to feel the effect of our prayers, and will have the opportunity to be or do things differently.

Second –when we pray for someone with faith and obedience to God, it changes us as well.

I have found I cannot pray for someone for very long without my heart changing toward them. I begin to see them through Jesus' eyes, and when I yield my heart, I begin to forgive.

I believe we've all heard it said, "When we forgive someone, it doesn't mean they were right, it just means we have forgiven their wrong doings."

We are then free!

Have you truly forgiven someone that had wronged you, and then you felt a heaviness lift off you?

Un-forgiveness is bondage, and it will literally make you sick!

I'm *not* saying every sickness stems from un-forgiveness. I *am* saying that long term anger, bitterness and resentment, which are all forms of un-forgiveness, have been proven to directly affect your health and your walk with God!

The Bible says God can't forgive us until we have forgiven others, and that includes forgiving ourselves. *"For if you forgive men their trespasses, your heavenly Father will also forgive you. But if you do not forgive men their trespasses, neither will your Father forgive your trespasses."* **Matthew 6:14-15**

The apostle James tells us in Chapter 5 verse 16, *"Confess your trespasses to one another, and pray for one another, that you may be healed. The effective fervent prayer of a righteous man avails much."* (NKJV) Righteous means one that is in right standing with God.

Although it's not usually easy to forgive, it is *possible* and **absolutely** necessary if we are going to have an effective prayer life.

Un-forgiveness will separate us from God and will most definitely hinder our prayers!

Isaiah 59:2 *"But your iniquities have separated you from Your God. And your sins have hidden His face from you, so that He will not hear."*

Isaiah 1:15 *"When you spread out your hands, I will hide my eyes from you; even though you make many prayers, I will not hear."* To spread out your hands means to pray.

After I became a Christian and knew I was called to be an Intercessor, things went along fine for a while but then it started to feel like my prayers were not reaching God!

It's interesting but it seems like a new believer starts out living their Christian life inside a "protective bubble", where any prayer they say is immediately answered. Then one day, without any warning, an Angel strolls by with a sharp pin, and 'pop' no more bubble!

It is now time to truly begin your walk with God!

"So God, I don't seem to be feeling Your Presence as much as I used to and my prayers feel like they crash against the ceiling, never going any further."

"What have I done Father?"

The Holy Spirit responded with, "It's something you *haven't* done."

"Oh, ok what do I need to do?" Gently Holy Spirit said, "Forgive them." I wondered who, although I didn't ask.

Holy Spirit answered anyway..." You know who." My response was a barely audible, "Yes, yes I do."

My reaction, to such an impossible suggestion was "But how can I?"

Remember when they did this and remember when they did that…I ranted on a few minutes more, reminding God how awful things had been and how I just couldn't see a reason to forgive them.

Finally when I became quiet, I heard the gentle voice in my heart say – "Pray for them. I love him."

Of course that's what God would say!

So began a lesson in God's unconditional love for everyone, which also included *them*!

"But I say, to love your enemies, bless those who curse you, do good to those who hate you, and pray for those who spitefully use you,

and persecute you. That you may be sons of your Father in Heaven; for He makes His sun to rise on the evil and on the good, and sends rain on the just and the unjust. **Matthew 5:44-45**

"For if you love those who love you, what reward have you? Do not even the tax collectors do the same? And if you greet your brethren only, what do you do more than others? Do not even the tax collectors do so?" **Matthew 5:46**

At first, I prayed out of sheer obedience to God, because I loved and trusted Him.

I didn't mean what I was praying.

I asked God to change my heart so my prayers would be real, and I could truly forgive.

I was persistent! I believed prayer causes situations, circumstances and people to change and brings God's will to pass in the earth.

Over time my heart began to change towards them. I started to see them through God's eyes, and finally my prayers were real, I meant what I prayed.

No, it was not easy, but it was possible!

I even had the opportunity to talk with them about salvation. They said they weren't ready. I asked God to place someone in their life that they would be willing to listen to. I prayed for them for several years before I finally felt the release to stop.

I don't know if they ever gave their heart to Jesus, but I do know that God will give them every opportunity to do so.

CHAPTER 14

FORGIVING OURSELVES

It was a part of my life I never wanted to think about ever again, so I had managed to bury the hurt pretty deep.

When the Holy Spirit spoke to my heart saying, "It's time to forgive yourself," I totally ignored His voice. Yep, that never works out well.

Holy Spirit showed me a human heart that for all outward appearances looked normal. (Some weeds are very pretty, and you don't really know they are weeds at all).

Under the surface the heart had a weed growing' This particular weed, however, had taken root and there were so many roots branching off, they are literally entwining and suffocating the heart, squeezing the life out of it.

This heart can no longer function the way God intended it to.

I believe the weed I saw represented un-forgiveness to myself.

Sharing about this is very difficult. I even took it out of this book and then put it back again.

Father, please let this bring peace to someone that is struggling with forgiving themselves. God will forgive…

Psalm 103:12 *"As far as the east is from the west, so far has He removed our transgressions from us."*

And God will forget you ever did it. He says He will…

Isaiah 43:25 "*I, even I, am He who blots out your transgressions for my own sake; and I will not remember your sins.*"

After the birth of my last child, my left leg had started hurting and gradually the pain had increased along with the leg becoming swollen and discolored. Two trips to the Dr. and no one seemed to know what was going on. Now I was at the ER, waiting for the nurse to bring me the papers saying I could go home. They still had no answer to what was wrong with my leg.

A GYN/OB doctor was seeing a patient in the next cubicle to me. She parted the curtain and said she had heard the conversation with the doctor who had just released me and was wondering if I had recently had a baby. I told her yes and within minutes I was admitted to the hospital.

The doctors suspected I had a blood clot and cautioned me that I had a 95% chance it would break loose and kill me.

As it turned out I *did* have a pulmonary embolism the next day, which means the blood clot broke loose and went through my lung. I prayed desperately for God to spare me, and He did. I was not born again but truly prayed a fervent prayer.... That's another story.

I had to tell you all of that, so this part would make sense.

When my son was almost a year old, I became pregnant again. My doctor said I had to have an abortion because the pregnancy would probably kill me. I was almost four months pregnant and refused to have an abortion.

I tried talking with my husband, but he agreed with the doctor, saying he didn't want to raise our 2-, 5-, and 8-year-old boys, and even possibly a new baby as well, by himself.

Then he said he would leave me if I continued to refuse the abortion.

At this point in my life I was a Catholic so I talked with my priest, hoping he would understand how I felt about my baby and the thought of an abortion!

But he even advised me to get the abortion assuring me since the doctor insisted, I needed the abortion that it would be the doctors' sin, not mine. Neither the priest nor my husband would listen when I said I would be killing our baby.

Father Ned said my first concern should be for my husband and three young sons that needed their mother!

I was so afraid! I knew I couldn't take care of four children if my husband left, and I was no longer sure he would even be there to care for them if I died!

So, here I am.

They just wheeled me into a room in the basement of the hospital, dimly lit, but I could still see the bare pipes overhead. What a dreary dark place. My heart seemed to match. The nurse said they would be back shortly to get me.

I wasn't yet a Christian, but I finally talked to God. I felt His presence and then I actually heard a voice that said, "Don't have the abortion, it will be ok." They hadn't given me any kind of medication yet, so I know it wasn't that. I heard the voice, not out loud but it was very loud all the same.

It wouldn't be until years later that I would realize it had been the Holy Spirit speaking to me.

Such a wonderful peace came over me, the first I had felt in weeks. Just minutes had passed when two nurses returned telling me I was next. They were going to give me something to make me sleep.

I calmly told them I had decided not to have the abortion and needed to speak with my husband so he could take me home. They refused to get him and held me down to give me the shot to sleep…I still hear my voice crying and saying no, no I don't want this…

The ride home is pretty much a blur as I kept fading in and out of consciousness.

By morning I was bleeding and having contractions. I found out later they had killed my baby, causing me to go into labor and abort it. At home.

My husband had gone to work so I was there all alone. My baby was born dead, and I ended up in the local hospital heavily sedated for 3 days. They said it would help my body and mind heal. My body did heal, my mind did not.

And life went on. Very few people even knew I had an abortion. The hurt and shame were too overwhelming to share.

No one even noticed I didn't want to hold any newborn babies. You know how people always want you to hold their baby? Well I just couldn't…it would tear my heart out if I held a baby.

Every year on my baby's due date, I would silently mourn for her. Yes, it was a girl.

I blamed the doctor, I blamed my husband, the priest, and the nurses that wouldn't listen to me. But more than anyone else, I blamed me. I had made the final decision to go to the hospital.

Gradually, I got back to living life. Everything seemed ok, even to me.

But God saw my heart, and the pain and un-forgiveness I had hidden so deep inside of it. And the weed that was squeezing the life out of it!

"For the Lord does not see as man sees; for man looks at the outward appearance, but the Lord looks at the heart." **I Samuel 16:7**

After I had received salvation, I had truly forgiven my husband, the priest, and everyone involved with the abortion. What I didn't consider was since I had always felt it was really my fault, I needed to forgive myself as well. And I hadn't.

Gently the Holy Spirit began showing me through His Word and through others, that I could forgive myself. Not only that I could, but I needed to!

When you are seeking God about forgiveness, always remember that it includes forgiving ourselves! Un-forgiveness is un-forgiveness.

Sometimes we blame God for something that we think He could have or should have prevented, instead of trusting that He always does what is best.

Always remember that God loves us, because of who He is not because of anything we did or did not do.

"*Father, forgive them, for they know not what they do.*" Jesus spoke those words recorded in **Luke 23:34.** KJV

I believe it is the greatest example of forgiveness there is!

Jesus endured the pain of betrayal, mockery, horrific beatings, and cruelty, adding to that the humility of being spit on!

Then the agony of total aloneness, as His Father turned His face away. "*My God, my God, why have You forsaken Me?*" **Matthew 27:46**

What had he done wrong? NOTHING! Did He deserve to be treated like that? NO!

He was innocent of any crime and totally sinless! He could have asked God to send 12 legions of angels (more than 72,000 angels) at any time! **Matthew 26:53** – Jesus says this, "*Or do you think that I cannot now pray to my Father, and He will provide Me with more than 12 legions of angels?*" and in **John 10:18 KJV** "*No man takes it from Me. But I lay it down of myself. I have power to lay it down and I have power to take it again.*" Jesus was speaking of His life.

But Jesus chose to forgive! Why?

Because He knew God, knew His Word, and chose to look beyond that time in His life to the fulfillment of God's promise to mankind and to Him!

He believed and trusted His Father. No matter what His circumstances were, He chose to forgive!

He chose to love!

How could any of us chose not to forgive another. No matter what they have done.

Even ourselves!

CHAPTER 15

ASK IN FAITH AND YOU SHALL RECEIVE

Hebrews 11:1 KJV *"Now faith is the substance of things hoped for, the evidence of things not seen."*

Faith is trust and confidence in God!

II Corinthians 5:7 KJV

"For we walk by faith not by sight."

I was 10 when I first realized God not only *heard* my prayers, but He *answered* them! I asked Him for what I thought was impossible and received it!!

I suppose every child at one time, or another has asked their parents for that little brother or sister. And some have probably asked Him to take a few of them back…just saying!

In my case I wanted a sister. I had a younger brother, and he was pretty cool, but I still wanted another girl.

In fact it was probably a good thing he didn't know what I had asked for since he was the youngest of 4, and the other 3 were girls. The older girls had moved out by then, so it was just my brother and me.

I asked my mom and dad if we could have just one more girl, a baby sister for me!

"No! Absolutely Not! There will be no more children, it's not even possible…and don't ask again!" When my parents said no, then it was no, and truly the end of the discussion!

I would pray every night, and as far as I know, I was the only one in my family that did. My little girl prayers of "Now I lay me down to sleep, I ask the Lord my soul to keep", had progressed to *big girl* prayers of God bless mommy, God bless daddy and on and on until I had asked God to bless everyone I could think of!

Then THE night came, yep, the night I realized He is God and He made people, right? Right!

So how hard would it be for Him to create for me one little baby sister? And since He was making her just for me, why not ask for the model I really wanted! Ok, blonde hair, blue eyes, dimples. That pretty much described my best friend, and *everyone* liked her.

It didn't matter to me that my parents, my brother and I were all dark haired and had hazel eyes, except my dad who had blue eyes.

He was God. I asked Him. I believed He would do it. And He did!

My little blonde haired, blue eyed, yes dimpled little sister arrived suspiciously close to nine months later!

Never underestimate the power of a child's faith!

Children simply take God at His Word. Their faith is strong.

Mark 11:24 KJV *"Therefore I say to you, whatever things soever ye desire when ye pray believe that ye receive them and ye shall have them.*

CHAPTER 16

THE APPOINTMENT

I awoke that morning, startled…my first thought was "Wow, what a dream that was!" Now even though I was completely awake, I still had the overwhelming fear that it wasn't a dream. I felt like I was going to Hell! I was terrified!

As you might imagine, I tried to ignore the feeling! As the day went on, I would suddenly become gripped by an overpowering fear! It felt as if there was a horrible black cloud "hovering" over me that would just not go away!

Needless to say, I was very confused!

So when my husband came home from work, I explained to him that even though I knew I had recently been saved *and* covered by the blood of Jesus, I still felt overcome by fear and the 'knowing' that I was most certainly headed to Hell!

He suggested we go together and talk with our Pastor. If I hadn't felt so much fear, I probably would not have gone to talk to him. After all, who wants your Pastor to know you're a flaky basket case, right?

Let me say right now, NEVER let the enemy convince you that you don't need wise and Godly counsel. You do! We all do!

I thank God that my husband was supportive! And I thank God as well for Pastor William Jenkins and his wife Cathy! Although at that time they were young in their ministry, they were wise in their counsel!

After re-establishing the certainty of my final home, Pastor Jenkins suggested that God was drawing me to pray for someone that was unsaved and fearful of eternity in Hell.

He said the 'feelings' I was having were those being felt by the unsaved person. I would have described them as a *lot* stronger than fearful, but the point was made!

Pastor Jenkins suggested that God was calling me to be an Intercessor!

I went home very much relieved I wasn't on a fast track to Hell!

My husband and I prayed together, asking God for His guidance, trusting that He would confirm to me that I was to be an intercessor. And what I should do next.

It didn't take God long!

Have you heard the expression that God will put 'feet to your prayers'?

Well the next morning I awoke to 'footsteps! Not really, in reality, it was the telephone, but footsteps none the less!

My Grandma in California was calling to tell me Grandpa was in the hospital, in a coma, and had been for a few days. She hadn't let me know so I wouldn't worry since I was so far away, but now they knew Grandpa wasn't going to make it. The fact was, the doctor was removing all life support the following day. As I hung up the receiver, I was once again overwhelmed with the terrifying fear of eternity in Hell. And I was sure no one could help me! I had chosen this path and now it was too late!

I knew then it was my Grandpa's heart I was feeling!

I heard the Holy Spirit say, "He's in a coma but his spirit man is very much awake...and aware!"

God worked out all the details. We had 3 young children and no money for the trip, but by that evening my husband and I were on the road to California.

We spent most of the trip praying and believing that even though the life support would be removed, God in His mercy would allow Grandpa to live until someone talked with him, and he could have one more opportunity to receive salvation. Even if it wasn't us.

I asked God why someone else couldn't have gone to the hospital and spoke to Grandpa? You know, someone at least in the same state, not several states away! He didn't answer. Back to that later...

We finally arrived at the hospital and were told by the nurse we could not go in to see Grandpa, only his immediate family were being allowed in. There was no one there visiting to even vouch for us.

"Why God?" "Why would You have us drive all this way if we are not to be allowed in to speak to him?"

God's answer – "I didn't" Take authority in Jesus' name and ask again." We bowed our heads and hearts to God and took authority over the situation in the name of Jesus.

A boldness rose in my spirit as I calmly explained to the person at the desk that we had driven hours and hours without stopping so we could see my Grandpa before he passed!

Well maybe the calmly part was a bit of an exaggeration *but in spite of me*, God, true to being God, changed that situation in an instant!

We were given permission to go in, briefly, since there were no other family members waiting to see him.

Thanking God first, and then the nurse, we went in to see Grandpa.

Entering the room, my heart broke to see my Grandpa, though still in a coma, he was thrashing about. Even though his eyes were closed, I could plainly see them frantically moving back and forth under his eyelids!

The gripping fear, panic, and now hopelessness I felt were overwhelming me!

Pastor Jenkins had explained to me that sometimes God will allow the Intercessor to "feel" someone else's pain and emotions, as if they are their own. Thus 'standing in the gap'.

I began praying in the Spirit as my husband took Grandpa's hand. He spoke to him by name, saying "God knows your heart Grandpa, and He's brought us here to help you. God loves you! I'm going to show you how to receive His salvation and give you the opportunity to accept His Son Jesus as your Savior."

He patiently and thoroughly explained to Grandpa how he could receive salvation. He spoke the scriptures out loud, confirming the truth about what he was saying to Grandpa. As he spoke, Grandpa began to relax and was thrashing about less. I could "feel" Grandpa's hope as it grew to become belief!!

Grandpa's body was in a coma, but his spirit was very aware – and that is who my husband spoke to when he said..." I know you can't say the words out loud, but you can say them in your heart, and if you mean them, then you *shall* be saved!"

He then told Grandpa he was going to say a prayer, and if he agreed with it, to repeat it in his mind. He told him God was reaching out to him and giving Grandpa the chance he had been asking for! An overwhelming peace, even stronger than the fear had been, settled over me, and filled the room as well! We could feel it! A total absence of fear!

The words of this scripture came to my mind – *"There is no fear in love; but perfect love casts out fear, because fear involves torment."* **I John 4:18**

A very audible sigh escaped Grandpa's lips. No more thrashing, no frantic eye movement, no fear! Only the gentle rising and lowering of Grandpa's chest as he peacefully rested.

The nurse appeared at the door, saying it was time to go. Smiling, we thanked her for allowing us our time.

We both told Grandpa we would see him again in heaven and I leaned over, kissed him on the cheek, and softly said, "Please tell Jesus thank you for me!"

Feeling a little drained, a whole lot tired, and so very happy in our spirits, my husband and I rode the elevator in silence. Before we arrived at the main floor, a Code Blue was called for ICU. We looked at each other with a "knowing" in our eyes and in our hearts. Grandpa was with Jesus!

And yes, the Code Blue was for him. Angels had *replaced* the demonic forces that *had* been waiting in the room for my Grandpa!

God is faithful when we are obedient!

Back to why us and not someone else closer to California, or even better qualified?

God's answer – "Because I asked YOU!" An intercessor needs an obedient heart.

I asked my Grandma if anyone had talked to Grandpa about salvation, and her answer, "You know your Grandpa, he probably wouldn't have listened if they had."

Our Father loves us so much He will do whatever it takes to bring us to Him and to salvation!

Except force us! We still have free will.

But He needs willing vessels, those who will say "yes", no matter what the cost.

To be the 'feet to the Intercessors prayer'.

I don't want God to find no one willing, do you?

"And I sought for a man among them that should make up the hedge, and stand in the gap before Me for the land, that I should not destroy it." **Ezekiel 22:30 (KJV)**

"Search me, O God, and know my heart, try me and know my thoughts and see if there be any wicked way in me, and lead me in the way everlasting." **Psalm 139:23-24**

"I call to You, Lord, come quickly to me; hear me when I call to You. May my prayer be set before You like incense; may the lifting up of my hands be like the evening sacrifice.

Set a guard over the door of my lips. Do not let my heart be drawn to what is evil so that I take part in wicked deeds along with those who are evildoers; do not let me eat their delicacies." **Psalm 141:1-4**

"Hear my prayer, O Lord, give ear to my supplications; in Your faithfulness answer me, and in Your righteousness. Do not enter into judgment with Your servant, for in Your sight no one living is righteous." **Psalm 143:1-2**

"Forever, O Lord. Your Word is settled in heaven! **Psalm 119:89**

CHAPTER 17

GOD SEEKS INTERCESSORS

Isaiah 62:6-7 – *I have set watchmen upon your walls, O, Jerusalem, who shall never hold their peace day or night. You who make mention of the Lord, do not keep silent and give Him no rest till He establishes and till He makes Jerusalem a praise in the earth.*

Isaiah 59:16 – *And He saw that there was no man, and wondered, that there was no intercessor.*

Isaiah 63:5 – *And I looked, and there was none to help; and I wondered, and there was none to uphold.*

Isaiah 64:7 –*There is no one who calls on Your Name, who stirs himself to take hold of You.*

Ezekiel 22:30 – *And I sought for a man that should stand in the gap before Me for the land, that I should not destroy it; but I found none.*

John 15:16 – *I chose you and appointed you, that you should go and bear fruit; that whatsoever you shall ask of the Father in My name, He may give you.*

These are just some of the scriptures showing us God wants to partner with man, through intercession, to accomplish His Will on earth.

As intercessors, our power comes through realizing we can do nothing of ourselves, but it is God's Spirit working through us. I am not saying we *do* nothing, totally the opposite! Because nothing is accomplished without prayer coming first.

Prayer causes situations and circumstances to change, bringing God's Will to pass in the earth.

It is in this nothingness of self that we receive the power in prayer.

We trust God, seek His heart, and speak His Word. When we petition Him in prayer, speak His Word over the situation and then have faith to see Him do it…He does it!

We often feel the pain, broken ness, and despair of those we are interceding for. We bring their needs and their petitions to God *for* them. We speak His Word over the person or situation, and we have the faith that He will do it.

We do all of that, *We* are standing in the gap for them…but it is *ONLY* God that brings the results and answers to their petitions.

WE do *nothing* of ourselves!

God wants you to take your place as His intercessor.

With the Helmet of Salvation firmly on your head, the Shield of Faith in place, so you can effectively withstand the fiery darts of the enemy!

To have your Sword of the Spirit drawn, defeating the enemy with the Spoken Word of God!

The Word of God is Truth, and the Truth will make the captive free. With Perseverance you must boldly *stand* your ground. We should never be discouraged about our intercession or wonder if it's accomplishing or changing anything. Of course it is!

It is God's Word and His Will being prayed into the lives of humankind. God called you to pray. He never said you would see the results of your prayers. Sometimes we do, sometimes we don't. It doesn't change the fact that God has answered our prayers!

TO ALL INTERCESSORS

AS YOU FIGHT THE SPIRITUAL BATTLE,

REMEMBER, WE CAN'T LOOK AT OUR OWN LIMITATIONS,

INSTEAD WE MUST LOOK AT GOD'S LIMITLESS POWER

THAT CAN WORK THROUGH US!

CPSIA information can be obtained
at www.ICGtesting.com
Printed in the USA
LVHW080358171022
730854LV00019B/236